SUPER
SURPRISING
TRiViA
ABOUT
RAIN FOREST
ANIMALS

by Megan Cooley Peterson

CAPSTONE PRESS
a capstone imprint

Spark is published by Capstone Press, an imprint of Capstone
1710 Roe Crest Drive, North Mankato, Minnesota 56003
capstonepub.com

Library of Congress Cataloging-in-Publication Data is available on the
Library of Congress website.
ISBN: 9781669050537 (hardcover)
ISBN: 9781669071693 (paperback)
ISBN: 9781669050490 (ebook PDF)

Summary: Think you know a lot about rain forest animals? Prepare to know
even more about the crazy, cool animals that swing from the branches,
swoop through the canopy, and creep along the dark forest floor. You'll be
surprised how much you'll discover in this totally terrific book of rain forest
animal trivia.

Editorial Credits
Editor: Erika L. Shores; Designer: Heidi Thompson; Media Researcher:
Jo Miller; Production Specialist: Tori Abraham

Image Credits
Alamy: Imagebroker, 16, Nature Picture Library, 17 (bottom), 25 (top),
Papilio, 17 (top), Science History Images, 29; Getty Images: DC_Colombia,
19, Jose Rui Santos / 500px, 20, Mark Newman, 27 (top), Westend61, 15
(top); Newscom: Paulo de Oliveira/NHPA/Avalon.red, 28; Science Source:
Francesco Tomasinelli, 12, The Natural History Museum, London, 14-15
(middle); Shutterstock: Adalbert Dragon, 10 (top), aDam Wildlife, 18, Allen
Lara Gonzalez, 8, Avector, 14-15 (bottom), cellistka, Cover (bottom right),
COULANGES, 26, Dan Olsen, 14 (top), Dirk Ercken, 9 (top left), Don Fink,
Cover (top left), Eray Bozkurt, 4, Eric Isselee, 11 (top), 27 (bottom), Ghing, 6,
haveseen, Cover (top right), Hollygraphic, (design element) throughout, Ian
Duffield, 23 (bottom), LedyX, 21, lessysebastian, 9 (bottom), Lukas Kovarik,
7 (bottom), Matyas Rehak, 7 (right), mexrix, (background) throughout,
nattul, 22, Nynke van Holten, 10-11 (bottom), Passakorn Umpornmaha, 7
(top), Pisut chounyoo, 13 (top), Rosa Jay, 9 (top right), Stefan Pircher, 24,
TERRESTRE, 13 (bottom), tristan tan, 25 (bottom), Vaclav Sebek, 23 (top),
Vasiliy Koval, 5, zebra0209, Cover (bottom left)

inted and bound in China. P05379

TABLE OF CONTENTS

Words in **bold** are in the glossary.

DID YOU KNOW?

Millions of strange and interesting animals live in **rain forests**. Some hang from trees. Others slip along the ground. Some have bright colors. Others blend in. What you discover about these animals may surprise you!

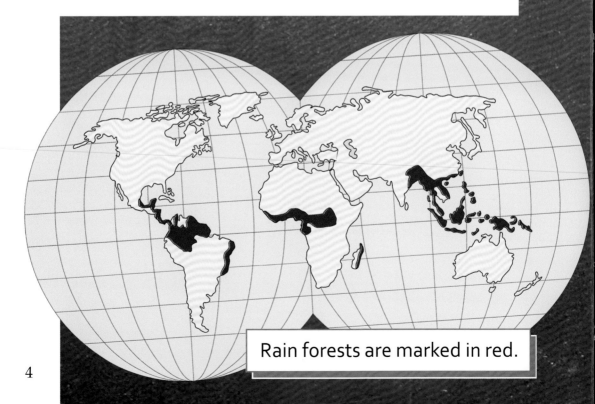

Rain forests are marked in red.

JUMPERS and CLIMBERS

Look! A tarsier has huge eyes.

Its eyes are bigger than its brain.

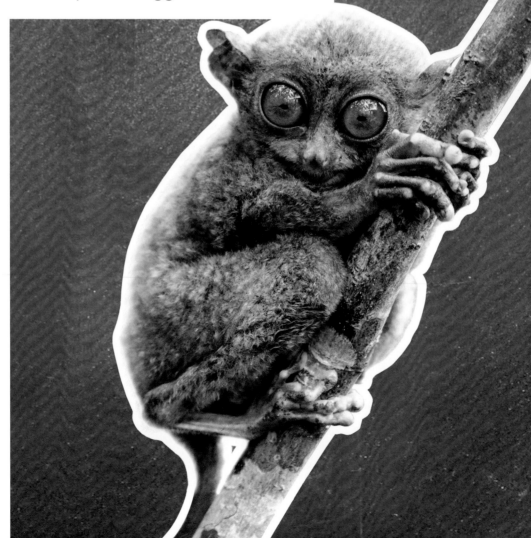

The world's largest **rodent** eats its own poop!

This helps **digest** all the grass a capybara eats.

Sloths are blind. They find their

way using their sense of smell.

Glass frogs have see-through skin.

You can see their hearts pumping blood.

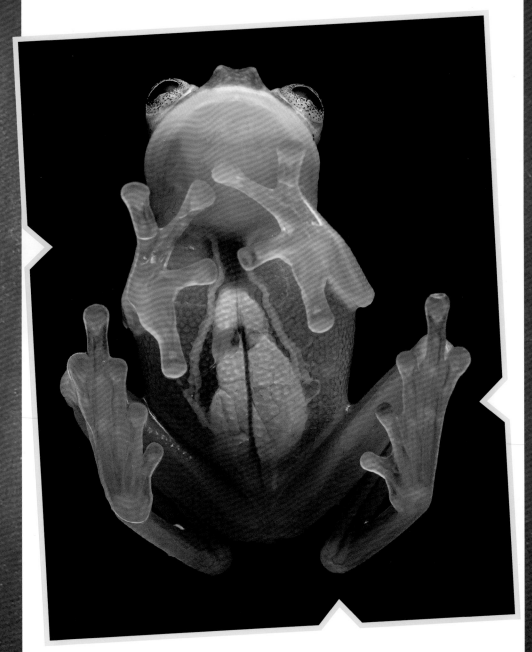

A poison dart frog's bright skin is toxic. The poison in one frog can kill 20,000 mice.

The Amazon milk frog's skin oozes poison when the frog gets scared.

Chomp! A jaguar's jaws can bite through an animal's skull.

Green anacondas are the biggest snakes on Earth. They can weigh up to 500 pounds.

A tapir's nose and long upper lip look like an elephant's trunk. These tiny trunks grab leaves to eat.

CREEPY CRAWLIES

The giant fishing spider walks on water. It can dive underwater and stay there for almost an hour!

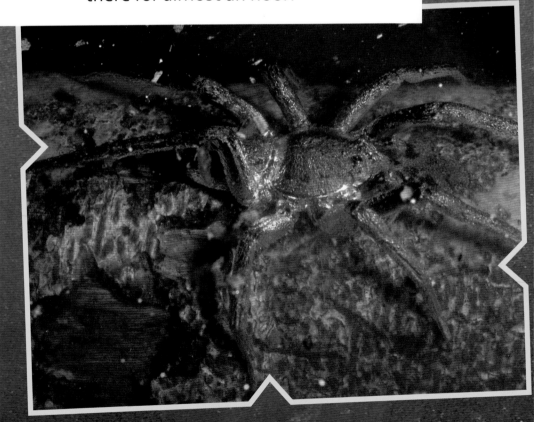

Rhinoceros beetles are the world's strongest animals. They can lift 100 times their own body weight.

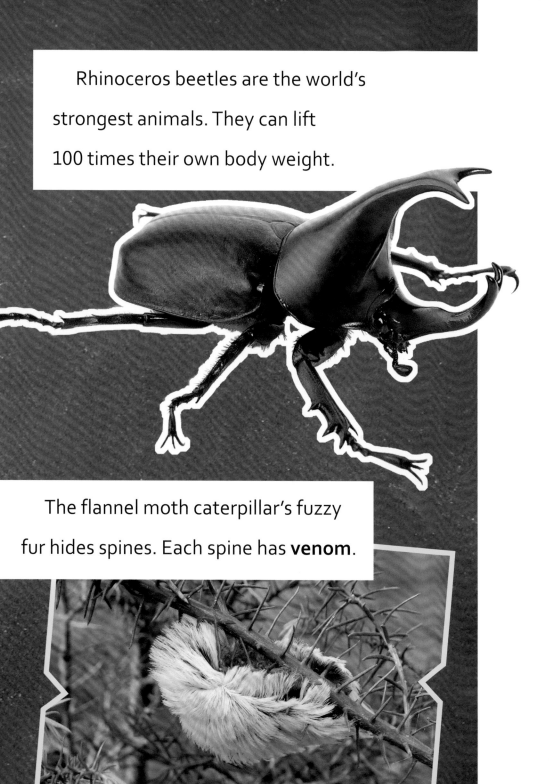

The flannel moth caterpillar's fuzzy fur hides spines. Each spine has **venom**.

Leaf-mimic katydids look like leaves.

Hungry animals pass them by.

Brazilian wandering spiders live on banana leaves. They sneak into banana boxes that get shipped around the world. That's why they are nicknamed banana spiders.

What is the length of a ruler? The giant centipede!

On guard! Male giraffe weevils smack their necks together like a sword fight. The winner **mates** with the female.

Goliath beetles are the biggest beetles on Earth. They are about the size of a tennis ball.

Bullet ants have the most painful insect bites on Earth.

UP in the AIR

Malayan flying foxes glide with wings 6 feet across.

Harpy eagle talons are bigger than a grizzly bear's claws!

The hoatzin is called the stinkbird.

Its breath smells like cow poop!

Blue morpho butterflies have brightly colored wings. Airline pilots can spot them from their planes.

The rhinoceros hornbill looks like it has two **bills**. The top horn is empty. This horn makes the bird's call louder, like a megaphone.

Red-capped manakin males shake their butts and show off yellow leg feathers. The females choose the best dancers!

The hyacinth macaw is the world's largest parrot. From head to tail, this parrot is longer than most house cats.

LURKING in the WATER

Most sharks live in saltwater. But bull sharks also live in **freshwater**. Some swim up the Amazon River.

Basilisk lizards run on water! They dash up to 65 feet in a single burst.

Electric eels build nests out of spit. It keeps their eggs from drying out.

River dolphins blush when they get excited.

Their pink skin turns even pinker.

The green anaconda speeds
through the water at 10 miles per hour.

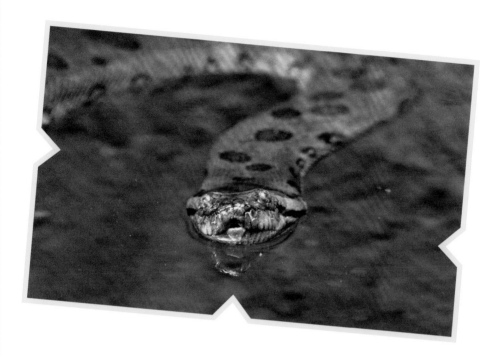

Mata mata turtles have long snouts.

They use them to breathe while swimming.

Most fish breathe with **gills**. Lungfish also have lungs. They cover their bodies with slime. They burrow into the mud and breathe with their lungs.

Payara fish have huge bottom fangs.

They are nicknamed vampire fish.

Glossary

bill (BIL)—the hard front part of the mouth of birds

digest (dy-GEST)—to break down food so it can be used by the body

freshwater (FRESH-wa-tur)—water that does not have salt; most ponds, rivers, lakes, and streams are freshwater

gill (GIL)—a body part on the side of a fish; fish use their gills to breathe

mate (MATE)—to join together to produce young

rain forest (RAYN FOR-ist)—a thick forest where rain falls almost every day

rodent (ROHD-uhnt)—a mammal with long front teeth used for gnawing; rats, mice, and squirrels are rodents

venom (VEN-uhm)—a liquid poison made by some animals to kill its prey

Read More

Light, Char. *20 Fun Facts About Forest Habitats*. New York: Gareth Stevens Publishing, 2022.

Pang, Ursula. *Beware the Poison Dart Frog!* New York: Enslow Publishing, 2023.

Sabelko, Rebecca. *Rain Forest Animals*. Minneapolis: Bellwether Media, Inc., 2023.

Internet Sites

Journey into Amazonia
pbs.org/journeyintoamazonia/index.html

Tropical Rainforest Information for Kids
rainforests.mongabay.com/kids/

Index

About the Author

Megan Cooley Peterson has been an avid reader and writer since she was a little girl. She has written nonfiction children's books about topics ranging from urban legends to gross animal facts. She lives in Minnesota with her husband and daughter.